Help, My Mind is Too Loud

How to Declutter and Quiet Your Mind

By: Dexter L. Scott

Copyright © 2022 by Dexter L. Scott, The UPgraders LLC

ALL RIGHTS RESERVED. No part of this book may be modified or altered in any form whatsoever, electronic, or mechanical, including photocopying, recording, or by any informational storage or retrieval system without express written, dated and signed permission from the author, except for the use of brief quotations in a book review.

ISBN: 979-8-218-00714-0

Graphic and Photo Credit: Jamar Hargrove

Contents

Acknowledgements 4

Introduction 6

The Primary Causes of Mindset Clutter 8

Environment/Surroundings 8

People 12

Distractions 16

Thoughts 20

Mindset Habits 21

Everyday Stress 22

Decisions 24

Unfinished Business 25

Dealing with Thought-Based Clutter 26

Breathing is the Key 26

Overcome Negative Thoughts 35

Clarify Your Purpose 37

Conclusion 40

Let's Stay Connected 41

Acknowledgements

This book is dedicated to my parents, Wilbur and Mamie Scott. While my father is no longer with us, his profound wisdom and life examples still resonate with me today. They both encouraged me to be the person GOD called me to be. I dedicate it to my amazing wife, Dr. Tonya Joyner-Scott who is an inspiration to me daily. Her love and support mean the world to me. I dedicate it to my children, Tailiah, Kiera, Morgan and Tyler who make me being their father a tremendous joy. I dedicate it to my son-in-love Adonis who is an amazing man who treats our daughter Kiera with the love and respect that makes us smile. I dedicate it to my granddaughters Ava and Erin who warm my heart with love every time I see them. I dedicate it to my in-laws, Henry and Peggy Battle. My father-in-law Henry is a beacon of strength, calm and has a demeanor that would put any situation at ease. We unfortunately lost my mother-in-law Peggy in April 2021 but she was the most incredible person I could have ever called mother in law. Her warmness, love and ability to bring joy to an atmosphere will greatly be missed. To my siblings, in-laws, aunts, uncles and mentors I have learned from all along the way, you are greatly appreciated. You all have played a significant part in my learning over the years and for that I am grateful.

It's time to declutter your mind so you can approach life from a clear perspective.

Introduction

If you are currently holding this book in your hands, I would like to say, thank you. This means a lot to me. Secondly, you are holding this book because you, just like me, have recognized that the world has entered into information overload. With the global pandemic over the last few years, our way of life has made a 360 degree change from anything we could have ever imagined. Just the thought alone can bring a degree of anxiety and stress. From the new normal of work from home office environments to dealing with colleagues and people on different platforms, our proximities have become a bubble. With all of this going on, we have an urgent need…the need to Declutter!

The word declutter doesn't just apply to the conditions of our homes. The closets, the pantry, the kitchen, and even the garage are places we automatically think about when we refer to decluttering.

It's much deeper than that. Decluttering most certainly can relate to our environment; but, what about what it's doing to our minds!

Decluttering can be applied to our mindset; however, something this important is what's not realized; and most of all, overlooked. What defines "decluttering"? By definition, *"It's the process of mentally organizing the necessary and eliminating the unnecessary clutter, worry and thoughts…"*

This can also be accomplished by making changes to your life and how you think. Although mindset clutter is always caused by your thoughts, external events and surroundings can serve as emotional triggers as well.

Eliminating those triggers is a powerful way to declutter and reclaim your mindset.

You can also have ineffective habits for dealing with stress, clutter, anxiety and uncertainty. Overthinking is definitely one of them. It boggles your thinking process and drains your ability to focus.

When we talk about environment and surroundings as possible sources of mindset clutter, these things really aren't conducive to a calm and relaxed attitude. Unfortunately, sometimes the people in our life can contribute to this dilemma.

It is important to address every possible cause. Let's take a deeper look into how we can reclaim our peace of mind.

*"When we clear the physical clutter from our lives,
we literally make way for inspiration and good,
orderly direction to enter."*
- Julia Cameron

The Primary Causes of Mindset Clutter

Environment/Surroundings

Your environment and surroundings include both your home and your work. You spend most of your time in one of these two places. *Now, don't make the mistake of underestimating the impact your environment and surroundings can have on your mindset!* Removing these clutters can have a positive effect on the negative thoughts going on between your ears.

Think about it, if you encounter anything that's counterproductive to getting things done, it can begin to pull on your subconscious activities in a way you don't even recognize. Your behavior changes, you become on edge, a number of things can happen. Even now as I write this, my wife and I are discussing ways we can declutter everything that concerns us. The pandemic forced a lot of people to start working from home and while some benefited, some saw it as a huge challenge to stay focused on tasks. Your desk(s) may have become a storage area for junk mail! If you have kids, most of them are doing remote learning which is an entirely new situation and it could feel that the walls are closing in on you. Even if you didn't switch to remote work, your office environment underwent significant changes. Nothing is off limits as it relates to being productive and getting rid of clutter.

As you read this, you are thinking of your environment right now aren't you?

In a time when we thought small things couldn't throw us off our game, we are seeing that it actually can. There are many factors within the work and home environments that can contribute to mindset. Your environment can play a critical role in how you deal with life challenges that we all face. For example, if your environment is cluttered and unorganized, whether it be physically, mentally or emotionally, you will feel cluttered. This negative mindset can drastically affect your daily tasks. In some instances your mindset can lead to a mental illness such as depression. Again, nothing is off limits.

Clutter can affect our anxiety levels, sleep and ability to focus. It can also cause us to withdraw from people or things that we care about. It can make us less productive, triggering how we cope with life's issues, and avoidance strategies. You start avoiding things that need to be done. What transpires from this is an avalanche of pressure. At some point, the pressure has to come out. Mindset helps you recognize that "there is an underlining problem".

Have you ever heard of an exercise called mind mapping? My wife and I use it often. It's the process of visually organizing information. It shows pieces of relationships in information that's hierarchical. I recently shared on Facebook Live how to use your mind to map out how to get to your nearest McDonalds!

Sounds funny right? But it's powerful and it works. Try it now. Enter your mind and SEE your direction to your nearest McDonald's. You begin to process in ways that many of us are not familiar with. A friend of mine sent me a YouTube video that very next day on mind-mapping that was absolutely incredible! (I'm not surprised he sent it;

because, when you realize the power of your R.A.S. (*Reticular Activating System*), you will know it was bound to happen! (That's another topic for another book.)

Anyway, the video gave some incredible information that I believe you will find useful as well. Just type in "Mind-mapping" on Google and you will find examples of how it works.

As it relates to decluttering your environment and surroundings, begin to organize your day in blocks of time. Utilize your smart phone to use the feature of 'Do Not Disturb'. Turn this function on for the period of time you want to focus and then itemize your to-do-list based on importance.

You've heard it said, "Eat the Elephant first?" The concept suggests breaking down large tasks into manageable chunks. Well, I agree with this to a certain extent. Getting those major tasks off to a great start is powerful, but can have a negative effect. If that elephant is incredibly large and your expectations are set on getting it completed in a specific time frame and you don't meet it, that's not an ideal situation.

However, if you itemize a quick win or two, you can feel incredibly accomplished by the feeling of having things crossed off the list before the focus time has ended. It's the same concept of making up your bed in the morning immediately when you get up. It starts your day with a quick win.

Begin to think of ways you can get your environment and surroundings back in balance. Then you can implement the things mentioned above to begin the decluttering process. As things are constantly changing in our world, and if you find yourself shifting again to return to your office environment, take these same concepts and ideas with you. They work and your adaptability to change will help you declutter and get that peace of mind you so much deserve.

"The first step in crafting the life you want is to get rid of everything you don't'."

- Joshua Becker

People

There are certain people that are hard to eliminate from your life. Your children are one example. No matter how old your children may be, the bond between parent and child is incredibly strong, as it should be. Whether it be children, parents, family as a whole or friends, it's sometimes hard to consider the next statement as truth: *Not everyone has a place in your life. Ouch…*

Your life is sacred. Be careful who you choose to include.

Consider how much the people in your life add and/or detract from it:

1.   Which people are a source of negativity? (This is important.) These people aren't negative about your life. They are negative about life in general. These are the people that are pessimistic, complain about everything, and suck the life out of you every time you see them. I have heard them called "Energy Vampires". Ask yourself this question, "Why do I keep them around?". There's an Einstein quote that says "Energy is everything and everything is energy". No wonder you are drained by certain people. You've allowed their energy to pollinate with yours! One of my favorite quotes of all time is "Where the mind goes, the energy flows". Look at it like this, your mind is caught up in a whirlwind of negative energy being around certain people! **Ouch** again… Now you get the point!

2.   Consider the toxic people in your life. Toxic people get in your way. They are the people that get in the way of you reaching your goals. They are discouraging, sabotaging and can throw off any positive energy. For some

reason, they feel better if you don't better yourself. We all know these kinds of people. One of my mentors has a quote that sums up toxic people, "You are either a great example or a terrible reminder". They are either inspired by you or don't like you because you remind them of what they could have been.

☐ It's rare to have people that truly want to see you excel. If you do, consider it a blessing! However, that's no reason to tolerate those who intentionally become obstacles in your life.

☐ *If it's a close friend or family member, first have a frank discussion.* If that fails to have an effect, then show them the door. It may be painful, but it's necessary. There is one thing that is vitally important and that's time! You can't get it back. Make sure to spend it with the right people.

3. Friends from another time. It might be an old college friend or a co-worker from 20 years ago. Do you have anything in common besides your past? How much enjoyment do you receive from them now? Think about it and make the necessary adjustments. Everyone changes and it's okay to understand that and move on.

4. Unfamiliar social media connections. You know these people. They are Facebook "friends" that are actually friends of friends of friends. Let's be frank, while it's special, do you need to see the birthday pictures of their grandchildren? Do you need to see what they ate for dinner last night? Do you need to see their constant post of nothing that concerns you? Social media has become a dumping ground for everything from jokes, to political hate, to absolute nonsense. How much of this do you really need? Know, also, that the "unfollow and unfriend buttons" can be your friend when you recognize how important your time is. Remember: Declutter! Allow in only what is necessary.

☐ If you are using social media to promote your business, the more the merrier. My wife Tonya and I use social media all the time but we have come to the conclusion that even that needs to be adjusted. Of course, it depends on which platform you are on; as some are driven towards more business related topics. Focus on what you are there for. Otherwise, make the necessary adjustments and stop wasting your valuable time.

5. Think about the people you work with. Fortunately or unfortunately based on how you look at it, you have fewer options here. You might be able to eliminate those non-productive people that work for you if you are a thriving business owner, but even that's not easy in today's day and age of uncertainty. You do have options. What about the company you work for? You can find another position within the same company or even leave your current company and find another. Have you heard the term, "Fire your boss"? Well, that's very true if your mind is constantly being cluttered with unnecessary things that don't improve you. Have you heard of the "Great Resignation?" With 47.4 million people having resigned their positions (according to CNBC) throughout the pandemic, there has to be a position out there for you that will match your goals and dreams. Do your due diligence and create the reality you want. Don't be afraid, be bold. Important Note: Start with decluttering your mind first.

Not everyone deserves to be part of your life. You only get one chance at life on earth so make the best of it. *Ensure you're not allowing the people around you to lower the quality of your life experiences.* Eliminate quickly those people that are unnecessary, bring you stress and anxiety and don't have your best interest at heart.

Make sure to provide time for people that will contribute to your life and happiness.

"As important as it is to learn how to deal with different kinds of people, truly toxic people will never be worth your time and energy - and they take a lot of each. Toxic people create unnecessary complexity, strife, and, worst of all, stress."

- Travis Bradberry

Distractions

Distractions can be clutter all by themselves. *Distractions are contributors to clutter and procrastination. It diverts your attention from what is important and allows clutter to grow even more.*

Procrastination is a self-created phenomenon that none of us are immune to, everyone faces it.

You never feel good while procrastinating. The work that you're avoiding is still hanging over your head and compiles. *No distraction is enough to completely eliminate that nagging feeling.* You continue to check the time, shifting your attention back and forth between the distraction and the work you should be doing. The result is debilitating mindset clutter.

Some distractions aren't all that distracting though. They just happen to be a more enjoyable option than the work you should be doing. Really think about the previous statement because it is powerful and telling at the same time. However, some distractions are highly distracting in their own right. Allow me to be brutally honest here; I'm a recovering Hallmark movie addict! Some days are more difficult than others; especially, around Christmas time. There, I said it. Let's move on (lol)

Let us evaluate the distractions you face in your life each day:

1.   How do you waste time? Forget about procrastinating for the moment. If you have nothing pressing on your schedule, how do you waste time? Make a list. A few popular culprits include:

- Social Media / Internet

- TV/ Streaming Services

- Cell phone-related activities

- Video games

- Shopping

- Mindless chatting with friends (Texting, etc.)

- These are likely the same ways you spend your time while procrastinating. **WOW!**

2.   Consider the cost of that lost time. Even if you only waste one hour per day, and it's likely much more than that, that is 365 hours per year. That is over nine 40-hour work weeks. That's over two months! Based on most statistics, we think 3,000 thoughts per hour, that's a whopping 1,095,000 thoughts! Think of what else you could do with all that time.

- Exercise

- Build an existing or new business

- Invest more in personal development courses

- Make new and better connections

- Write a book in your field of interest

- Learn a new language

- Learn to play an instrument

- Spend more time with loved ones

- Remember! You likely waste a lot more than 60 minutes each day!

3. Make a list before going to bed. Prepare a list of the most important 3-5 tasks you have to do the following day. Ensure that at least half of your list are items that will move your life forward in some way. Bedtime is the perfect time to do this because you are literally dropping seeds into a fertile ground which will begin to germinate overnight. It's a very powerful concept.

4. Understand why those items are important. Understand the benefit you're gaining by taking these actions. Like my father use to say, "There's nothing like a good understanding". Knowing why is the beginning of a solid exercise.

5. Reduce each task to the necessary steps. Tasks that are too big or too poorly defined encourage procrastination. Remember when we discussed the elephant? Challenge yourself, but also get the quick win.

6. Reduce your distractions. Remove any from your environment. Turn off your phone or use the do not disturb feature. Turn off the internet if you don't need it for your work. Unplug the television or put the remote up. Shut the door to your office. Place ear buds in your ears. Lock yourself in a bare closet if you must. These may seem drastic, but quieting your mind will require it.

7. Set a timer. Unless you've been meditating in a cave for the last ten years, you can't expect yourself to be able to concentrate for 8 hours straight. Data even suggests that the average adult attention span has reduced from 12 minutes to 8 minutes! This means Goldfish have a longer attention span than most humans. We are doomed for clutter if we don't change. Use a timer to

create time boundaries. *Most of us can concentrate for 30-60 minute blocks at a time.* Then take a break for 5-10 minutes and get back to it.

Distractions are everywhere. Some of us are naturally better at ignoring distractions than others. I recall talking with my uncle, a retired United States Navy Captain and he is one of the most athletic men I know. He described to me how he would run 5 miles daily, come home, shower and get right to work at his office desk. Here's the kicker, he worked around 3 toddlers constantly needing his attention and screaming all at the same time. He is one of those fortunate individuals who can ignore distractions. For me, that's not the case. What about you?

Use your time to the best of your ability by reducing the distractions in your life. You're then in a stronger position to avoid procrastination. Set yourself up for success.

Consider that the worst procrastinators you know are struggling the most with life. Procrastination is perhaps the greatest fertilizer for a loud, uncontrollable mind.

> *"Elegance is achieved when all that is superfluous has been discarded and the human being discovers simplicity and concentration: the simpler and more sober the posture, the more beautiful it will be."*
>
> \- Paulo Coelho

Thoughts

Your thoughts are the genesis of mindset clutter. This is where it all starts. *Get control of your thoughts, and your mindset clutter will be tamed.* This is a major task, and not for the faint-hearted! It can be done, though. My uncle said to my wife and me many years ago, "You can't keep a bird from flying over your head but you can keep him from building a nest". The faster you can control your thoughts will set the precedence for everything that follows.

There are several things that affect your thoughts.

They include:

- Mindset habits (Familiar neuropathways- things that happened during your childhood)

- Everyday stress

- Making decisions, especially when there are too many options

- Unfinished business

Mindset Habits

Like your actions, many of your thoughts are habitual. You think about the same past experiences over and over. You daydream about the same imagined future over and over. These thoughts may be positive or negative, but they still contribute to mindset clutter. As a matter of fact, 95% of what you are thinking today transferred over from yesterday and 80% of those thoughts are negative.... **OUCH.**

Here are a few mindset habits that provide little benefit:

- ☐ Guilt
- ☐ Worry
- ☐ Regret
- ☐ Comparing yourself to others (Social Media)
- ☐ Gaining self-esteem by pleasing others
- ☐ Mentally checking out when faced with stressful situations
- ☐ Worry what others think of you
- ☐ Expecting the worst
- ☐ Thinking about the past and the future

Really contemplate whether you struggle with any of these negative mindset habits and start making the adjustments as soon as possible.

Everyday Stress

This is a big one. *Your mind fills with clutter as your stress level increases.* Fight or flight kicks in. Your thoughts become less controlled and more negative. It's not surprising that many serious mental health issues are often precipitated by stressful events. It's like a train that has run off the tracks and can't stop. The level of stress that you face each day is relevant to the amount of mindset clutter you have. I remember reading a story of the late Attorney Johnnie Cochran. He was on his way to one of the highest profile cases ever, the O.J. Simpson trial, and something weird happened. He encountered someone who had a flat tire. He pulled over, pulled off his jacket, changed the tire, put his jacket back on, and finished driving to the trial. WHOA! Think about it. If he didn't know how to manage stress, he would not have even considered pulling over to assist due to pressures of the trial.

It's often the accumulation of little things that have a significant impact on our lives. It could be traffic, late bills, your child has a runny nose, you and your spouse are at odds, or even being late for work can send your brain into a tailspin. Too many smaller stressors can be just as stressful as large stressors. Remember that. Once we understand what is happening to us, we can begin the process of arming ourselves with the right processes to help us succeed in reclaiming ourselves.

"The greatest weapon against stress is our ability to choose one thought over another."

- William James

Decisions

Making a lot of decisions can really wear you out and create mindset clutter. There's a reason why Steve Jobs, Former President Barack Obama, Mark Zuckerberg and Albert Einstein limited their daily wardrobes to just a few items – the elimination of choice.

A phenomenon known as "Decision Fatigue" kicks in and even the smartest people succumb to silly decisions. It's a fact.

When you're faced with too many decisions, mindset clutter grows and can spin out of control.

Studies also show that making decisions decreases your ability to make additional decisions. Eliminate as many possible decisions as you can each day.

Here's a really good thing about habits. Habits eliminate the need to make a choice. Stick with the same healthy breakfast and take the same route to work each day. If you don't have habits, get them fast!

Use habits to your advantage and save your decision-making muscles for important decisions.

Unfinished Business

Often the result of procrastination or indecisiveness, unfinished business takes up valuable mindset space as well. It may be the phone call or text you need to make. Or, it could be cleaning up your house, organizing your office, finishing your taxes, or just getting the oil changed in your car. It can be EVERYTHING!

These things can seem trivial in the short-term, but there's a price to be paid each day. Notice how much better you feel when you complete these responsibilities. Again, remember the small wins.

"Being in control of your life and having realistic expectations about your day-to-day challenges are the keys to stress management, which is perhaps the most important ingredient to living a happy, healthy and rewarding life."

- Marilu Henner

Dealing with Thought-Based Clutter

There's good news! *All your mindset clutter is ultimately self-induced.* Fortunately, that means that your mindset clutter is under your control. It also means that you don't have anyone to blame besides yourself. Again, **OUCH**!

Breathing is the Key

The process of breathing is pretty amazing and we have taught it often. It's the only bodily function that you can consciously control or have done for you automatically. You can breathe more deeply or more shallowly on command. Fast or slower isn't a problem either. Your Autonomic Nervous System runs the show. On the other hand, you can forget all about breathing and it still happens. Imagine that!

An adult at rest takes roughly 20 breaths per minute. That's over 28,000 breaths per day. Most of those breaths happened without any intention on your part. You weren't even aware of at least 99% of them.

The cycles of breathing, Beta, Alpha, Theta, Delta and Gamma. Once you learn them, it could change your entire life. That's truly amazing.

Maybe breathing is the secret to managing your thoughts! Hmmmm.

There are two ways breathing benefits mindset clutter:

1.   Changing your breathing can change your physiology. Try breathing faster for a minute and notice how you feel. Now breathe very deeply for a minute and notice the changes. Changes to your breathing change your physiology. Changing your physiology can change your thoughts and your focus.

2.   Focusing on your breath can keep your mind in the present moment. Your breath is your thread to the present. No matter how distracted you are by your thoughts, focusing on your breath can bring you back to reality. This is a very powerful exercise. For the last year, I have been getting up at 5:22 a.m. EST every morning to take our daughter to her first bus stop. Without fail, as I begin to drive down to road, my mind begins to process. This presents an issue because my desire is to come back home, get back in bed by 6 a.m. and rest for at least another hour before starting the day. When I get back in bed, it sometimes takes an hour just to drift back off to sleep. I must admit, this is an ongoing process. I have; however, found a hack that's been working for me. And, it could work for you! Pick a word, any word that gets your attention. My word is "Clear". What has been working for me is when I begin my drive and my mind starts to take off, I say in my mind "Clear" as many times as possible to erase the thought. Sometimes it requires me to say it out loud. Every time my mind starts I literally take action to shut it down. Find your word. Make sure it's a word that can "straighten you up" as they say. A word that calls your attention back to the present and stay in that zone until you are ready to start the thinking process. Give it a try, you will be happy that you did.

Breathing doesn't seem too exciting, but it is a powerful tool. What could possibly be simpler? There is; however, a skill component to using your breath in your clutter-reducing efforts. It will take time and patience to develop fully. Be patient with yourself, trust the process and enjoy the journey to wholeness.

Use your breath to alter your physiology:

1. Find a quiet place, if possible. If you are at work, close your office door or head for the bathroom. The more solitude you can find, the better. If you are home, this can be even better as you can control your environment more. *This technique will work anywhere, especially with practice.*

2. Get into a comfortable position. Seated is best. Ideally, you can assume a position that you can maintain for at least five minutes without moving. Try not to lie down as you may fall asleep.

3. Inhale slowly and deeply through your nose. Allow your stomach to expand. You're not trying to breathe so deeply that you feel pain. Just take a full breath. Feel the air pass by the tips of your nostrils. Then relax and allow the air to expel naturally. We always teach our clients to be consciously conscious.

☐ Avoid overcomplicating the technique. *Full, slow, and easy breaths are the objective.* Paying attention to your breath for just 5 to 10 minutes can be enough to feel a significant reduction in both your stress level and mental clutter. Take your time and build up to this point. Don't sweat it. Remember, the goal is to declutter your thoughts and mind.

This simple technique can be used anytime you are feeling stressed or your mind is cluttered. You can receive many of the same benefits as meditation by using these techniques.

This focused breathing technique can be used in the car, during a meeting, or any time you need to gain back control of your racing brain. The goal is to keep this exercise at the top of your mind to implement.

Meditation is the next logical step. Meditation is like focused breathing on steroids. It's more than just a quick-fix. It can literally transform your life.

There are many scientifically-proven benefits to meditation:

1.	Meditation decreases depression. Meditation has been shown to reduce obsession on one's discomfort and distress. In other words, you spend less time thinking about your challenges. This leads to a lower incidence of depression.

2.	Meditation increases the ability to regulate your mood. We have some control over our moods, just not as much as we'd like. You can probably think of someone in your life that regulates their moods very poorly. You never know what you're going to face when you see them. They have very little control when life happens to them. Meditation enhances the ability to manage your moods.

3. It decreases anxiety. Both emotional and physical stress markers are reduced in those who meditate.

4. It increases the ability to focus and work under stress. This can be one of the biggest benefits to those who meditate to declutter their mind. Remember the Johnnie Cochran story? I'm not sure but he definitely had some techniques of dealing with stress.

☐	It's not easy to sit still for an extended period of time and maintain your focus. As that ability grows, you can apply it to other areas in your life.

5. Meditation increases resilience. You'll be overwhelmed less frequently and find it easier to continue during times of stress.

There is a nearly endless list of the benefits provided by regular meditation. But it's obvious that meditation is a great tool to declutter your mind. *When you are in a better mood, you are less stressful, and you are able to focus. Your mind is less cluttered! This is a wonderful beginning of a different life.*

There are many types of meditations that people often use in order to have some control over how they handle what life has to bring from day to day.

Mindfulness meditation is an excellent choice for those who want to declutter their thoughts. This type of meditation is based on observations. You're not thinking, evaluating, or interpreting your thoughts. There is no judging involved. This is powerful!

You are just paying attention in a particular way. You can apply it during a variety of activities.

These include:

- Driving (remember my story)
- Eating
- Cleaning
- Showering
- Mowing the lawn
- Using your phone

- Sitting outside

While some forms of meditation attempt to limit thoughts, mindfulness meditation simply notices the thoughts that appear. This is great for beginners, because limiting your thoughts is very challenging! I'm an advocate of this method because of its power and effectiveness.

Mindfulness meditation is a simple, yet challenging, process:

1. Assume a comfortable seated position. A chair is fine. The floor is also an acceptable option. Comfort and support are key. Just like breathwork preparation, don't get too comfortable and fall asleep.

2. Become aware of your surroundings. Notice the temperature of the room. Notice the physical sensations of your feet, hands, back, neck and every other part of your body. Notice what you can see in the room. What do you hear? Be consciously conscious.

- Avoid judging anything. Even labeling isn't permitted. For example, you might be drawn to some artwork or piece hanging on your wall. It's not even appropriate to say to yourself, "I really like that or I remember when we purchased it." Saying anything, good or bad, about it isn't any better! Avoid even saying to yourself what color it is. Just observe…nothing else.

- *Keep your thoughts limited to what you can see, hear, and smell.* If you even hear a dog barking next door and remind yourself that you don't like the dog, you are not being mindful. Just notice the dog barking. That's it.

- It's surprising how relaxing this can be. Just notice and keep your brain's big mouth shut. *Do this for five minutes to start.*

3.   Turn your attention to your breath. Feel the breath throughout your body. Start at the nostrils and notice the movement and sensations of your chest and abdomen. Keep your attention on the part of your body where the breath is most easily felt. This practice has tremendous power.

- Continue this until the end of the meditation. Strive for at least 20 minutes, total.

The late Bob Proctor has an amazing meditation on YouTube that you should watch. It is amazing and it taps into this kind of breathwork activity.

4.   Notice your thoughts. Invariably, it won't take too long before you realize that you're thinking about your next meeting, who may be trying to call or text you, what you are having for dinner tonight or the next task you need to get done. That's okay. Again, avoid labeling your thoughts at all costs to accomplish the exercise. The following are unacceptable during this activity:

- "This is really weird."

- "Why did I think about that?"

- "What's wrong with me?

- "I think I'm going crazy."

- As with the sights and sounds in your environment, notice the thought without taking the next step of judging or labeling. Remember to be patient with yourself as you learn.

5.   Return your awareness to your breath. It's that simple.

Over time, you'll find that your thoughts, judgments, and tendency to label things will decrease. *The result is a decrease in your mindset clutter.*

Even consider how much mental noise you generate each day. It's astounding how much noise our minds conjure up. Imagine walking from your car into a retail store that you like. The temperature is 90 degrees outside. Think about the conversation you might have in your head.

- "It is really hot today."
- "Did the weather man say it was going to be this hot?"
- "I can't wait to get into the store where the air conditioner is on."
- "I like her outfit. I wonder where she got it from?"

Your mind can go on and on, right! Labeling things in our environment is a habit that accomplishes little to nothing. You don't need to say that it's hot outside. You already know it based on the sweat running down your face! You don't need to comfort yourself by saying to yourself that you'll be in the cool a/c in just a minute. You already know!

Meditation helps to quiet this unnecessary mental noise. *When you stop generating mindset chatter, you can deal with the real clutter in your life much more effectively.* You will be amazed at how capable you really are.

"Meditation is difficult for many people because their thoughts are always on some distant object or place."

- Wayne Dyer

Overcome Negative Thoughts

Are you plagued by mindset negativity? Do you say negative things to yourself? Do you worry about the future? Do you criticize yourself and spend too much time focusing on what you lack? That's natural for many of us; and yes, it sucks.

Scientists have a theory to explain all this negative thinking.

It was imperative a long, long time ago to human survival at the beginning of time. Unfortunately, it's not helpful to us anymore.

There was a time that food was scarce in the world. A member of another tribe might beat you to death with a club just for looking at his significant other. There were dangerous animals roaming around. Those that were overly cautious and worried about such things survived more often than those with a more relaxed, decluttered attitude. The crocodile brain was in full effect. Wow, times have changed!

Now, we have grocery stores, police, and most of the predators aren't an issue anymore. We have armies to fight in conflict and wars. We have all the luxuries now that we use to not even dream of.

Your negative thinking is something you inherited. However, it no longer serves you. Please understand this. Once you identify this type of thinking, now we are talking about a real paradigm shift.

Deal quickly with your negative thoughts:

1. Please understand that your negative thoughts are hurting you. Ninety-nine percent of your worries and negative self-talk are harming you. Believe this simple fact and you're halfway to freedom.

2. Be observant. Your new meditation skills will be helpful. Notice when you're having a negative thought. Again, remember to be consciously conscious.

3. Distance yourself from the thought. If you think to yourself, "I'm not good enough," shift your mindset to "I'm having a thought that I'm not good enough. That is not who I am". **Boom!**

    This simple process puts space between you and the thought. You realize that it's something separate from you and not you. This is something we teach in NLP (Neurolinguistic Programming) and it's very powerful.

4. Replace the thought. Reverse-engineer the thought. Tell yourself that you are good enough. Tell yourself that things will be okay. Is it true? Well, it's no more of a lie than telling yourself something negative. At least you will feel better and be in a better position to succeed. *Considering that things usually work out, it's more accurate than your negative thoughts. It's time to get in the driver's seat of your thoughts. Take control, my friend.*

"There is a plan and a purpose, a value to every life, no matter what its location, age, gender or disability."

- Sharron Angle

Clarify Your Purpose

Indecisiveness can be the result of a lack of clarity. Clarity if vital. *If you are unclear about your values and your goals, you will lack purpose.* You have been developing your values since childhood. They undergo modification as you age and develop new perspectives on life. Who we are, by the age of 19, has already been developed by 95%. This tells us that who we are now is a combination of life's experiences. Our values, our thoughts, even our mindset. When you think about it, adults are formatted children walking around every day and living our lives based on things that happened to us a long time ago, good and bad.

But you've probably never really given your values and experiences much thought. Now is the time to take a hard look. Keep in mind, this part of the journey is not sexy; but, it is needed. Your values play a big part in clarity. In NLP, we also study a process called Values Elicitation, which discovers what your current values are, as well as, discovering what makes you tick the way you do.

Take some time and determine your values and make easier, more congruent decisions:

1. Determine what is most important to you in life. Ask yourself this question and see what pops up. Here are a few examples to get your mind churning:

- ☐ Truth
- ☐ Tolerance

- ☐ Success
- ☐ Service to humanity
- ☐ Discipline
- ☐ Humility
- ☐ Happiness
- ☐ Family
- ☐ Generosity

This is just a small sampling to give you some ideas. Make your own list.

2. Reduce your list to just 6 values. Which are most important to you? What do these values mean to you? Don't rush this, take your time. If it is easier, start by eliminating those values you know aren't as important as other ones.

3. Are you living your life according to these values? Consider these parts of your life:

- ☐ Career
- ☐ Relationships
- ☐ Social life
- ☐ Family life

Do these parts of your life reflect your true values? If not, why? How would your mindset clutter be affected if you changed your life to reflect your values? This question is deep. Think about it, you can deal with unnecessary clutter when things are meshing together.

By defining your values, it becomes much easier to make decisions and set appropriate goals. When your life is in alignment with your values, your level of mindset clutter will decrease. Adjust your life and activities to match your values.

The next step is to create goals that keep your values in mind. Know your desired outcome and create goals to support that outcome. An example of this would be saying you want to be a millionaire, but you value your home and family life more than burning the midnight oil behind your desk. Your work ethic doesn't match up with your desire. Remember to be authentic to what's important to you. *When your values, goals, and life purpose match, the resulting synergy makes everything easier, and your efforts become more effective.*

> *"Don't dwell on what went wrong.*
> *Instead, focus on what to do next.*
> *Spend your energies on moving forward*
> *toward finding the answer."*
>
> *- Denis Waitley*

Conclusion

Many of the issues we deal with in life are due to loud minds and mindset clutter. You might have a great life living in your dream home, wonderful career, happy family, and a lot of other great things, But…

Your mindset clutter can be enough to eliminate all of those wonderful things. Yep, it's that important!

There is good news though…your mindset clutter is under your control and you can do this!

Address all factors contributing to your mindset clutter. Pay attention to your environment and surroundings, the people in your life, and the distractions. These triggers create the mindset clutter referenced in this book. Ultimately, your thoughts and mindset habits are your biggest culprits. Focused breathing, meditation, and addressing negative thoughts are the most powerful tools in your arsenal, so make sure you use them. Keep everything in the above pages at your disposal so you can decrease the clutter and create the mental peace you so deserve.

Let's Stay Connected

Dexter is a sought after motivational speaker and he and his wife Tonya own a personal development company called The UPgraders. They are frequently asked to speak on platforms and train corporations, organizations, churches, businesses and groups on mindset development, communication and a plethora of tools that help people elevate in their lives on every level.

Dexter is available for speaking engagements. For booking information, please visit his website below.

Additionally, below are ways to connect with the UPgraders to elevate and excel in life and learn the strategies and tools that will expedite your process.

- Website: www.dexterlscott.com

- The UPgraders Academy Inner Circle (Membership Based Organization) - https://theupgradersacademy.com/

- The UPgraders: www.theupgraders.com

- Email: info@dexterlscott.com and info@theupgraders.com

- The UPgraders Youtube Channel: https://www.youtube.com/theupgraders

- 'Upgrade Your Life' podcast: bit.ly/theupgraderspodcast (also found on Google, Stitcher, Pandora and IHeart)

- Social Media: @dexterlscott on all major platforms (FB, IG, Twitter) Linked In: https://www.linkedin.com/in/dexterlscott/

www.ingramcontent.com/pod-product-compliance
Lightning Source LLC
Chambersburg PA
CBHW070520090426

42735CB00012B/2847